History of America

The Making of Modern America

1948 to 1976

Sally Senzell Isaacs

Heinemann
LIBRARY

First published in Great Britain by Heinemann Library,
Halley Court, Jordan Hill, Oxford OX2 8EJ,
a division of Reed Educational and Professional Publishing Ltd.
Heinemann is a registered trademark of Reed Educational & Professional
Publishing Limited.

OXFORD MELBOURNE AUCKLAND
JOHANNESBURG BLANTYRE GABORONE
IBADAN PORTSMOUTH NH (USA) CHICAGO

HISTORY OF AMERICA: THE MAKING OF MODERN AMERICA
was produced for Heinemann Library by Bender Richardson White.

Editor: Lionel Bender
Designer: Ben White
Assistant Editor: Michael March
Picture Researcher: Pembroke Herbert and Cathy Stastny
Media Conversion and Typesetting: MW Graphics
Production Controller: Kim Richardson

03 02 01 00
10 9 8 7 6 5 4 3 2 1

500 587558

Printed in Hong Kong

British Library Cataloguing-in-Publication Data.
Isaacs, Sally Senzell
  The Making of Modern America, 1948–76. – (History of America)
  1. United States - History - 1945– - Juvenile literature
  I. Title.
  973.9'18

ISBN 0431 05632 3 (Hb)   ISBN 0431 05638 2 (Pb)

Acknowledgements
The producers of this book would like to thank the following for permission to
reproduce photographs:
Picture Research Consultants, Mass: pages 6 (Library of Congress/R.Lee),
8 and 9 (Associated Press/World Wide Press), 12 (NASA), 14 (Associated
Press/World Wide Press/Bill Hudson), 15 (The National Archives), 21, 25
(Associated Press/World Wide Press/Sal Veder), 32, 34. Peter Newark's
American and Military Pictures: pages 17 (Dallas Times-Herald/Robert Jackson),
19, 23, 33, 37. CORBIS/Bettmann: pages 7, 20, 24, 26 (UPI), 31 bottom, 39.
CORBIS: pages 11 (The National Archives), 13 (Hulton-Deutsch Collection), 18
(Photoplay Archives), 29 (Sandy Felsenthal), 31 top (Leif Skoogfors), 35, 36, and
41 (all Charles E. Rotkin), 38 (Adam Woolfitt), 40 (Morton Beebe, S.F.). NASA:
page 28. VinMag Archive Ltd: pages 16, 27.

Artwork credits
Illustrations by: John James on pages 8/9, 12/13, 14/15; Gerald Wood on
pages 6/7, 20/21, 24/25, 26/27, 30/31, 32/33; James Field on pages 10/11,
16/17, 18/19, 22/23, 28/29, 34/35, 36/37, 38/39, 40/41.
All maps by Stefan Chabluk.
Cover design and make-up by Pelican Graphics. Artwork by John James.
Photos: Top: Picture Research Consultants (Associated Press/World Wide
Press/Bill Hudson). Centre: Picture Research Consultants (NASA). Bottom: Picture
Research Consultants (The National Archives).

Special thanks to Mike Carpenter, Scott Westerfield and Tristan Boyer at
Heinemann Library for editorial and design guidance and direction.

For more information about Heinemann Library books, or to order, please phone
01865 888066, or send a fax to 01865 314091. You can visit our web site at
www.heinemann.co.uk

Any words appearing in the text in **bold, like this**, are
explained in the Glossary.

Major quotations used in this book come from the following
sources. Some of the quotations have been abridged for
clarity.

Page 8: King's quote from *Martin Luther King, Jr The Dream
of Peaceful Revolution* by Della Rowland. Englewood Cliffs,
NJ: Silver Burdett Press, 1990, page 60.

Pages 8 and 9: Rosa Parks's quote from *Rosa Parks: My
Story* by Rosa Parks with Jim Haskins. New York: Dial
Books, 1992, page 115–116.

Page 16: Johnson's speech from *Four Days: The Historical
Record of the Death of President Kennedy* compiled by
United Press International and American Heritage Magazine.
New York: American Heritage Publishing Co, Inc, 1964,
page 39.

Page 20: Chavez quote from *A History of US: All the People*
by Joy Hakim. New York: Oxford University Press, 1995,
page 147.

Page 22: Johnson's quote from *Public Papers of the
Presidents: Lyndon B. Johnson – 1965*. Washington, DC:
Government Printing Office, 1966.

Page 22: King's quote from *Where Do We Go From Here:
Chaos or Community?* by Martin Luther King Jr New York:
Harper & Row, Publishers, 1967, page 86.

Pages 24 and 26: King's quote and Stokely Carmichael's
words from *Martin Luther King, Jr The Dream of Peaceful
Revolution* by Della Rowland. Englewood Cliffs, NJ: Silver
Burdett Press, 1990, pages 120 and 118.

Pages 26 and 27: King's Memphis speech and Coretta
King's public speech from *My Life with Martin Luther King Jr*
by Coretta Scott King. New York: Holt, Rinehart and
Winston, 1969, pages 316 and 327.

Page 28: Astronauts' quotes from *Apollo Expeditions to the
Moon* edited by Edgar Cortright, Washington, DC: NASA
1975, page 350.

Page 33: Nixon's resignation speech from *The Memoirs of
Richard Nixon* by Richard Nixon. New York: Grosset &
Dunlap, 1978, page 1,083.

The Consultants

Special thanks to Diane Smolinski, Nancy Cope
and Christopher Gibb for their help in the
preparation of this book.

CONTENTS

ABOUT THIS SERIES

History of America is a series of nine books arranged chronologically, meaning that events are described in the order in which they happened. However, each book focuses on an important person in American history, so the timespans of the titles overlap. In each book, most articles deal with a particular event or part of American history. Others deal with aspects of everyday life, such as trade, houses, clothing and farming. These general articles cover longer periods of time. The little illustration at the top left of each article is a symbol of the times. They are identified on page 3.

▼ About the map

This map shows the United States today. It shows the boundaries and names of all the states. Refer to this map, or to the one on pages 42–43, to locate places talked about in this book.

About this book

This book is about America from 1948 to 1976. The term America means 'the United States of America', or the US. Until around 1960, most African Americans referred to themselves as Negro. The word means 'black' in Spanish and Portuguese and refers to the dark skin colour of many African Americans. During the 1960s, people wanted to express pride in their colour and origins and chose to refer to themselves as Blacks, Afro-Americans or African Americans. Words in **bold** are described in more detail in the glossary on page 46.

INTRODUCTION

In 1948, most American citizens were proud of their powerful country. They had helped win World War II in 1945. By 1948, most people had jobs, homes and more extra time for leisure. But White Americans could not be proud of the way they treated their fellow-citizens, the African Americans. African American people could not apply for many of the jobs that White people had. In the southern states, they could not sit in the same section of a bus, restaurant or cinema with White people. African American children could not attend the same school as White children.

Martin Luther King Jr risked his life to bring about change for African Americans. For twelve years, he led one of the most important **revolutions** in American history: a revolution towards **equality.** King did not believe in fighting a bloody revolution. Instead, he wanted a peaceful revolution without violence. He organized marches where thousands of people gathered to express their unity and their demands. His powerful speeches gave African Americans pride and courage. Eventually, he helped change laws and behaviour. His life was a symbol of hope.

Many of the events in this book took place during King's life. On pages that describe events in his life, there are yellow boxes that tell you what he was doing at the time.

MARTIN LUTHER KING JR

As a young child, Martin Luther King Jr never paid attention to skin colour. Some of his neighbourhood friends were White. Others had dark skin like his own. One day, at the age of six, Martin learned that his skin colour mattered to many people. It was a lesson he never forgot.

Martin had run across the street to play with his friend. The boy's mother answered the door with a strange look on her face. She told Martin that he could not play with her son any more because Martin was 'coloured' and her son was White. The woman may have thought that Martin was not good enough to play with her White child.

Martin was surprised. He wondered, how could skin colour matter? His parents later explained things to him. Skin colour mattered to many people. That was why Martin's school had only African American children.

Martin Luther King Jr
Born: 15 January 1929
Father: Martin Luther King
Mother: Alberta King
Martin Jr skipped two years of high school and entered Morehouse College, an all-Black school in Atlanta, at the age of 15. In 1948, he graduated college, became a minister and left for Crozer Seminary in Pennsylvania to study religion. This was his first experience living in the North, where he was free to eat in restaurants and sit in cinemas alongside White people.
Martin Jr married Coretta Scott in 1953. They had four children. In 1955, he received his Doctorate degree from Boston University and was then called Dr King.

▲ Martin Luther King Jr was born in this house at 501 Auburn Avenue in Atlanta, Georgia. He lived here with his parents, grandparents, brother and sister.

▲ This African American is drinking from a water fountain to be used by coloured, or Black, people. This sign on the wall of the street-cleaning terminal in Oklahoma City shows that there is a separate water fountain for White people.

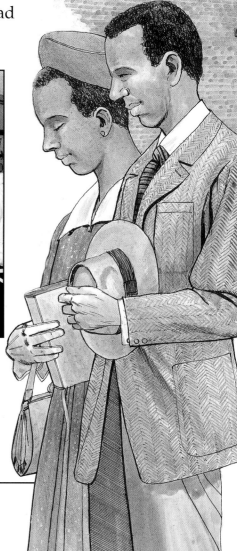

◀ Martin gave his first speeches in church. At the age of 25, he went to this church: Dexter Avenue Baptist Church in Montgomery, Alabama. Here he stands in a red gown in the doorway of the church.

▲ Martin Luther King Jr stands between two other religious leaders on 18 May 1956. They are attending a prayer service to celebrate the second anniversary of the **Supreme Court's** decision to outlaw **segregated** schools.

A long struggle

This inequality in America was not new. From the 1600s to 1865, millions of African Americans were forced to work as **slaves** on farms in the South. After slavery was outlawed in 1865, African Americans struggled for opportunities to work, find homes and get an education. Many southern White people disliked people who were different from themselves. 'Whites Only' signs hung in restaurants, cinemas and employment offices.

A powerful voice

As a teenager, Martin Luther King Jr knew he was a powerful speaker. He chose his words wisely. His voice was deep and strong. His words would change the attitudes of every American.

WALKING TOGETHER

Martin Luther King Jr felt he could end the unfair treatment of African Americans. He encouraged his people to fight – without violence. If a law was unfair, he told them to break the law – even if this meant going to prison. If enough people did this together, they would show that the law must change.

On 1 December 1955, in Montgomery, Alabama, a woman named Rosa Parks followed Dr King's suggestion. She boarded a bus and sat in an empty seat in the 'Black' section. At the next stop, some White passengers got on. There were no seats left. The driver told the African Americans to give up their seats to the White people. Rosa Parks stayed seated. "The more we gave in, the worse they treated us," she wrote later.

The bus driver pulled over and called the police. Parks was arrested for breaking a law that said Black and White people cannot sit together on city buses. Lawyers from an organization of African Americans called the **NAACP** rushed to the prison. They were glad that Parks broke the law. Now they would appeal to a higher court to prove the law was unfair.

Empty buses
The NAACP asked Dr King to lead a **boycott** of the buses. He persuaded Black people to stop riding buses. For over a year, Black people gave each other lifts in their cars or walked while empty buses roamed the streets. The boycott ended when the **Supreme Court** said buses could not be **segregated**, or separate Blacks and Whites.

Meet hate with love
King paid a high price for his beliefs. He received hate letters and threatening phone calls. One day, he came home to find that his house was bombed. Luckily, his wife and children were safe. As a crowd of Black supporters gathered around his house, he said to them: "If you have weapons, take them home. We must meet violence with non-violence. We must meet hate with love."

▼ By 4 September 1957, all state schools had to allow Black students to attend. Here, White students at a high school in Little Rock, Arkansas, are shouting insults at this African American student. In **protests** like this, National Guard and federal troops got involved on both sides.

► King read everything he could about Mohandas Gandhi (right). In the 1930s and 1940s, Gandhi led the people of India in **non-violent** protests, such as boycotts. Gandhi's leadership helped India gain independence from Britain.

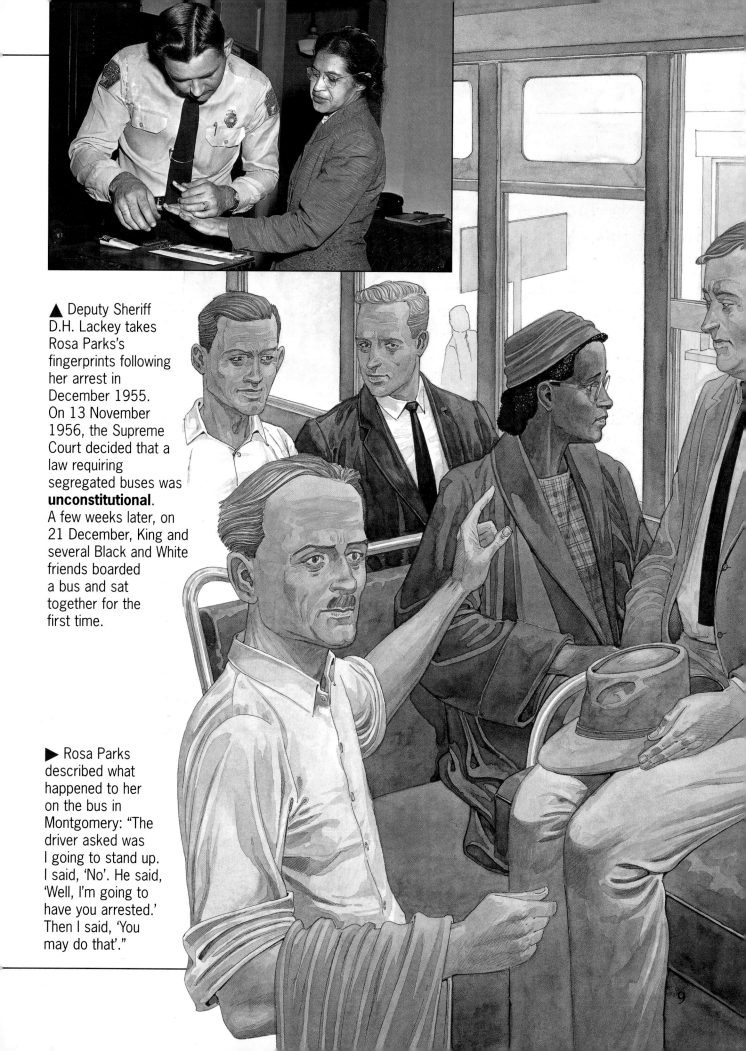

▲ Deputy Sheriff D.H. Lackey takes Rosa Parks's fingerprints following her arrest in December 1955. On 13 November 1956, the Supreme Court decided that a law requiring segregated buses was **unconstitutional**. A few weeks later, on 21 December, King and several Black and White friends boarded a bus and sat together for the first time.

▶ Rosa Parks described what happened to her on the bus in Montgomery: "The driver asked was I going to stand up. I said, 'No'. He said, 'Well, I'm going to have you arrested.' Then I said, 'You may do that'."

THE KOREAN WAR

During World War II, the United States and the Soviet Union fought together against a common enemy: Hitler's Germany. After the war, the US and the Soviet Union were the two most powerful countries in the world. But their governments were different. The US believed in capitalism and free speech. The Soviet Union did not.

The US has a **democratic** government. The people choose their leaders in **elections**. They enjoy freedom to speak out against their government. The **Soviet Union** had a **communist** government with central control. It held elections, but only one person ran for each office. Soviet people had free schools and hospitals, but could not criticize their own government.

After World War II, each country wanted other countries to follow its system of government. This struggle became a war in the Asian country of Korea.

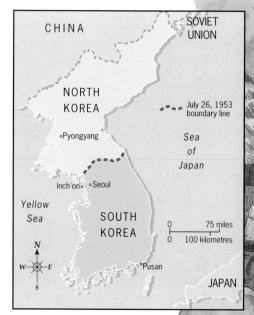

▲ Following World War II, South Korea became non-communist. North Korea became a communist country. During the Korean War, each side tried to take over more land. On 26 July 1953, a boundary line was set up.

► The struggle between communist and democratic governments was called the Cold War. Armies did not fight the Cold War. Instead, it was fought with words and threats. During the Cold War, Senator Joseph McCarthy of Wisconsin accused many Americans of joining the communist party. Although he had little proof, he accused army and government officials, authors and film stars. Many of these people lost their jobs.

◀ Between 1946 and 1958, the US tested **nuclear** bombs on two of the Marshall Islands in the Pacific Ocean. Against their will, the islanders were moved so they would not be affected by the harmful **radiation** of the bombs.

◀ During the Korean War, communist troops fought United Nations troops from 16 countries. On land, soldiers fired guns and tanks. Jet aircraft battled in dogfights overhead. Helicopters took the wounded to hospitals.

Fighting in Korea

The Soviet Union took control of the northern half of Korea. The US supported a non-communist government in the southern half. In 1950, North Korea attacked South Korea. The Soviet Union sent guns to North Korean soldiers. China, another communist country, sent soldiers. The **United Nations** sent troops to help South Korea defend itself. Most of those soldiers were Americans.

In 1953, the two sides agreed to end the war. More than 54,000 Americans lost their lives in Korea. Thousands of soldiers from other countries also died. Today, North and South Korea are still two separate countries.

◀ The US Navy sent ships to fire at North Korean cities. During the war, the Navy lost five ships.

THE TELEVISION ELECTION

49th and 50th states
In 1959, the United States acquired two more states: Alaska and Hawaii.

By the early 1950s, Americans were in love with TV. In these early days of television, Americans laughed at comedy shows such as *I Love Lucy*. They were thrilled by American heroes such as Superman and Elvis Presley. By 1960, many Americans were choosing a president based on the way he looked on the TV screen.

▼ On 20 February 1962, John Glenn Jr entered his spacecraft, *Friendship 7*, at Cape Canaveral, Florida. He became the first American to orbit Earth. His flight lasted five hours.

In 1960, John F. Kennedy was elected president. He was 43 years old – the youngest president ever elected. This was the first **election** in which Americans watched the candidates on TV. There were four TV **debates** between Democrat John Kennedy and his Republican opponent, Vice President Richard Nixon. Kennedy was more charming than Nixon. While Nixon seemed awkward, Kennedy seemed confident. Many people believe TV helped Kennedy win.

Kennedy's ideas
Kennedy had many new ideas. He set up the Peace Corps. It was made up of volunteer doctors, teachers, carpenters and farmers. These Americans lived among people in developing nations and helped in their communities.

Kennedy also encouraged America's space programme. The **Soviet Union** had sent the first man to **orbit** Earth in April 1961. In May 1961, Alan Shepard became the first American in space. In February 1962, John Glenn orbited Earth. President Kennedy announced that America would send a man to the Moon by the end of the decade. This goal was met in 1969, though Kennedy did not live to see it.

▲ In August 1961, East Germany built the Berlin Wall to separate East and West Berlin. West Germany had a **democratic** government. East Germany was **communist**. The Berlin Wall stopped East Germans from escaping to the West.

Sit-ins
From 1960 to 1962, Martin Luther King Jr encouraged **non-violent demonstrations**. He sometimes joined 'sit-ins' in which Black students sat at restaurant counters where they were not allowed. Angry White customers poured ketchup and hot coffee on the **protesters**. In a sit-in in Atlanta, Georgia, King was arrested and sent to prison for breaking **segregation** laws.

▲ A family watches a Nixon–Kennedy debate. Candidates now reached many more people through TV than they could by traveling from city to city. In 1950, only 10 percent of American homes had TVs. By 1960, 90 percent had them.

◀ These Cuban soldiers were training to fight against the US. In October 1962, President Kennedy learned that the Soviet Union was building **missile** bases in Cuba, 150 km from Florida. He sent out warships to stop Soviet supply ships. It looked as if there might be a war between the US and the Soviet Union. Then the Soviet ships turned back.

THE DREAM

Dr King met with President Kennedy several times. He persuaded the president to ask Congress for new civil rights laws. These laws provided for equal job opportunities for all and required public places, such as restaurants and hotels, to serve all people regardless of race, religion, sex or national origin.

African Americans wanted to be sure that the president and **Congress** knew the importance of the suggested **civil rights** laws. On 28 August 1963, more than 250,000 people gathered in front of the Lincoln Memorial in Washington, DC. Nearly 60,000 of them were White. It was the largest **demonstration** in the history of the country. That day, Martin Luther King Jr gave his most famous speech, in which he said:

"I have a dream that one day on the red hills of Georgia, sons of former **slaves** and sons of former slave owners will be able to sit down together at the table of brotherhood....I have a dream that my four little children will one day live in a nation where they will not be judged by the colour of their skin but by the content of their character."

A powerful new law

The following year, Congress passed the Civil Rights Act of 1964. This law said that all people must be treated equally, regardless of their **race**, sex, religion or national origin. Although this new Civil Rights law met King's approval, changing the feelings and habits of many Americans would not prove easy.

▼ In May 1963, thousands of African Americans, including hundreds of children, marched for freedom in Birmingham, Alabama. The city's police and firefighters stopped them with powerful fire hoses and snarling dogs. The scene was sickening, but it did not stop more marchers the next day. Again, the police and firefighters were ordered to attack. This time, they did not. With tears in their eyes, they let the marchers pass. King later wrote: "I saw there for the first time...the power of **non-violence**."

> **The road to civil rights**
> •1865 13th Amendment ends slavery
> •1896 **Supreme Court** says that African Americans could be kept out of White hospitals, state schools, toilets and waiting rooms as long as there were 'separate but equal' places for them. These places, however, were usually of much poorer quality.
> •1954 Supreme Court outlaws **segregation** in state schools
> •1960 Civil Rights Act increases safeguards of voting rights for Blacks
> •1964 Civil Rights Act ends the segregation of people in public places.

▼ Over 250,000 people listened to Dr King's 'I Have a Dream' speech. Many more watched on television. The speech gave Americans courage and hope.

▲ President Kennedy was a popular leader who served just 2 years and 10 months.

▼ The world was shocked when Kennedy was shot on 22 November 1963. He and his wife, Jacqueline, were riding through Dallas, Texas, waving to the people who came to see them. Suddenly, shots rang out from a nearby building. Within a few hours, Kennedy was dead and Vice President Lyndon Johnson became president.

THE GREAT SOCIETY

A few hours after Kennedy died, President Johnson stepped off the plane in Washington, DC. He stood before television cameras and spoke to the country: "This is a sad time for all people. We have suffered a loss that cannot be weighed....I will do my best. That is all I can do. I ask for your help – and God's."

Like Kennedy, Johnson wanted to help poor Americans. His plan for change was called The Great Society.

In November 1964, voters **elected** to keep Johnson in office. During his first two years, he encouraged **Congress** to pass more than 50 new laws. One of Johnson's most important programmes was called Medicare. The government would help pay the hospital bills of citizens over the age of 65. A programme called Medicaid helped pay medical bills for poor people.

▼ In the 1960s, many Americans enjoyed comfortable lives in the **suburbs**. Here are many appliances that made their lives easy. Despite the kitchen conveniences, Americans flocked to a new chain of fast-food restaurants called McDonald's.

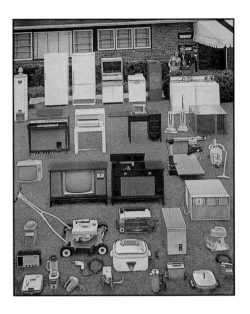

Across America
There can never be just one definition of 'an American'. The country is huge and the people live many kinds of lives. In the 1960s, while some city neighbourhoods had beautiful homes, other neighbourhoods were run-down. Many African Americans held good jobs in business and government. Many others had low-paid jobs or no jobs at all. Many were tired of waiting for Dr King's **non-violent** plans to work. In many cities, angry Blacks burned buildings and looted stores.

▼ In the 1960s, many university-age students believed in 'flower power' – the idea of changing the world through peace and love.

▼ In 1965, the US doubled the number of men **conscripted** into the army in order to fight in an Asian country called Vietnam.

▼ The US space programme was in full swing. Thousands of scientists worked for **NASA**. A Moon-landing was their objective.

The government's 'war on poverty'

As part of Johnson's Great Society plan, the government set up job-training programmes for poor people and gave loans to businesses in poor sections of cities. It set up programmes to build houses for people with low and middle incomes. It also started a preschool programme called Head Start to teach reading and maths skills to children in poor neighbourhoods.

In the 1960s, many **immigrants** came to America from Mexico, Puerto Rico and Cuba. These Hispanic Americans became the second largest minority, or separate group of people, in the US. Many started businesses in Florida or took jobs in factories in the East. People from Mexico did farm work in the West. Like African Americans, Hispanics did not have equal opportunities in finding housing and jobs.

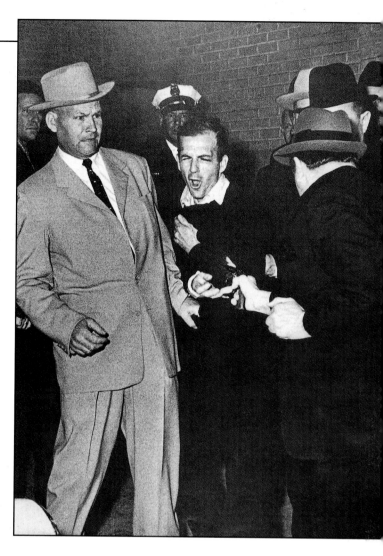

▼ These people live in government-built flats. The rents are low because the government pays for upkeep of the buildings.

▼ Life in a suburb included driving to dancing lessons and baseball games. Neighbours earned about the same money.

▼ By the mid-1960s, African American, Hispanic American and White American students all attended school together.

▲ Just two days after President Kennedy was killed, Americans faced another shock. Kennedy's accused killer, Lee Harvey Oswald (in the centre of this photo), was being led by police out of the Dallas city prison. The police were taking him to the county prison. TV cameras focused on Oswald and millions of Americans watched. Jack Ruby, a Dallas nightclub owner, stepped forward and shot Oswald. His bullet killed Oswald and kept Oswald's reasons for killing the president a mystery forever.

THAT'S ENTERTAINMENT

In the early 1960s, children loved the newest toys: Barbie dolls and hula hoops. Teenagers swooned to the songs of Elvis Presley, the Beatles and the Beach Boys. Parents assumed that their children would grow up to be just like them. By the mid-1960s, many young people did not want to be like their parents.

Americans seemed to choose sides. There were the adults – sometimes called 'the establishment' – who made the rules. There were the young people – many called 'hippies' – who wanted to break the rules. The hippies grew their hair long and spoke of solving the world's problems with peace and love.

In music, adults still liked the songs of such singers as Frank Sinatra. For youngsters, the 1960s brought 'rock 'n roll'. This music was part rhythm and blues, which was popular with African American singers. It was also part country music, which was popular with White singers. Rock 'n roll music was enjoyed by Blacks and Whites together. 'Pop (popular) music' boomed.

▲ Elvis Presley was America's first and most popular rock 'n roll superstar. When he appeared on Ed Sullivan's TV show in 1956, 54 million people watched. In 1964, when the British rock 'n roll group the Beatles appeared on the show, 70 million viewers tuned in.

▶ Teenagers of the early-1960s ate at drive-in restaurants.

▼ People carried transistor radios. This was the start of miniaturization of electronics.

America's games

In 1961, baseball player Roger Maris hit 61 homeruns, beating Babe Ruth's record set 34 years before. Maris's record stood until 1998 when Mark McGwire hit 70. In 1962, Wilt Chamberlain set records on the basketball court. He scored 100 points in one game and 4,029 points for the season. Michael Jordan, in his best year, 1987, scored 3,041. In Houston, Texas, the world's first indoor sports stadium opened on 9 April 1965. Baseball and American football were played in the Astrodome in all weathers.

◀ By the late 1960s, many young people **protested** against the rules and ways of life of the 'establishment', as shown on this magazine cover. Folk singers, such as Bob Dylan and Joan Baez, wrote songs about making the world more peaceful.

◀ In 1962, Telstar, the world's first commercial communications **satellite**, sent live TV pictures from one continent to another.

LIFE — THE YOUTH COMMUNES — New Way of Living Confronts the U.S. — JULY 18 · 1969 · 40¢

19

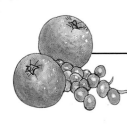

PROTESTS ACROSS THE LAND

"How long will it be before we take seriously the importance of the workers who harvest the food we eat?" This question was asked by Cesar Chavez. While California farm owners made good money selling their crops, the field workers who planted and picked the crops were homeless and hungry.

When Cesar Chavez was 10 years old, his parents lost ownership of their farm in Arizona. His family packed up the car and travelled from farm to farm in the West. If a farm owner had crops to pick, the family stayed for the season. They lived in a tent. They earned very low wages. It was a tough life. The children went to a new school every few months. By the time Chavez was a teenager, he had attended 38 schools. Nearly 30 years later, he decided to help **migrant farm workers** have a better life.

▶ Many Mexican Americans were migrant farm workers. They picked strawberries in the spring, then moved north to pick oranges, lettuce, and grapes.

▶ Native Americans also worked to improve their lives. In the 1960s and 1970s, they set up groups to demand that the US government honour past **treaties**. This photo was taken on 7 March 1973, at Wounded Knee, South Dakota. These two Oglala Sioux were among 200 Native Americans who gathered on the land that was once Sioux homeland to show that the government had not paid what was promised.

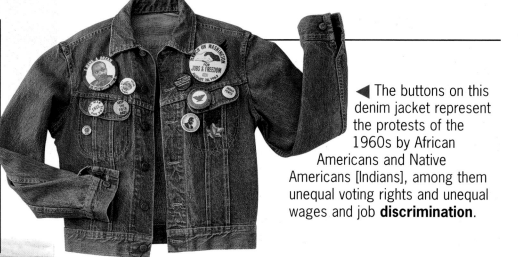

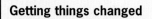

◀ The buttons on this denim jacket represent the protests of the 1960s by African Americans and Native Americans [Indians], among them unequal voting rights and unequal wages and job **discrimination**.

Getting things changed
Marches and protests brought various changes.
• In 1963, the Equal Pay Act required equal pay for equal work.
• The **Civil Rights** Act of 1964 said that an employer could not deny a person a job because of his or her sex, **race**, religion or national origin
• The 1965 Voting Rights Act prohibited southern states from barring Black citizens from voting.
• The Civil Rights Act of 1968 stopped discrimination in the selling or renting of houses and flats.

Unions and boycotts
Chavez wanted to force farm owners to pay their workers more money. He also wanted farm workers to have safer working conditions. Like Martin Luther King Jr, Chavez believed in **non-violent protests**. Starting in 1962, he travelled from farm to farm, talking to workers. He organized them into a **union**. If they acted together, they might convince farm owners to make changes. Workers held strikes in which they stopped working until the crops began to rot in the fields.

Chavez also asked people across the country to **boycott** California grapes. Many people agreed to stop buying these grapes until workers got better wages. Changes came slowly, but eventually farm owners agreed to pay higher wages and provide safer working conditions.

THE VIETNAM WAR

American soldiers once again entered a battle on another continent. This time it was in an Asian country called Vietnam. North Vietnam was run by communist leaders and supported by the Soviet Union. South Vietnam was non-communist.

In the 1950s and early 1960s, Presidents Eisenhower and Kennedy sent weapons and supplies to help the South Vietnamese soldiers. They wanted to stop the spread of **communism**. By 1965, President Johnson decided to send American soldiers also. Eventually, more than 500,000 Americans soldiers went to Vietnam.

Television brought the war into American homes. Terrifying pictures of burning villages and dying soldiers stirred up many feelings. Why did the United States have to fight another country's war? President Johnson said: "We fight because we must fight if we are to live in a world where every country can shape its own destiny. And only in such a world will our own freedom be finally secure."

▼ Vietnam is located in south-east Asia, near China. In 1954, the country was divided into North Vietnam and South Vietnam. This map shows the situation during the Vietnam War, 1965–1973. In 1975, the two sides united under a communist government.

King opposes the war
Martin Luther King Jr was against sending American soldiers to Vietnam. King disliked the violence of war. He also felt the $70 million a day spent on guns and bombings could be better spent on programmes to help the poor people in America. He wrote: "It challenges the imagination to contemplate what lives we could transform [change] if we were to cease killing."

▶ American soldiers arrive at a Vietnam battlefield by helicopter. They will fight in steamy jungles where the enemy could be hiding anywhere. They will have to kill and try to stay alive.

Map:

- CHINA
- Red River
- Hanoi
- Gulf of Tonkin
- BURMA
- HAINAN
- LAOS
- NORTH VIETNAM
- Mekong River
- N W E S
- ✳ Major Battle sites
- •••• Communist Trail
- SOUTH VIETNAM
- THAILAND
- Bangkok
- CAMBODIA
- Phnom Penh
- Saigon
- Gulf of Thailand
- South China Sea
- Mekong Delta
- 0   400 miles
- 0   500 kilometres

▼ This photo from 1967 shows a US soldier using a machine gun against North Vietnamese troops.

A costly war

By 1966, South Vietnam depended more and more on US weapons and soldiers. Much of the ground-fighting took place in thick jungles. Americans used bombs and chemicals to try to clear the jungles. In doing so, they permanently destroyed some of South Vietnam's farmland and plant and animal life.

By the time the last American troops left Vietnam in 1973, the US had spent over $150 billion. The US had dropped more bombs on Vietnam than on Germany and Japan during World War II. About 58,000 US soldiers had died and 300,000 were wounded. South Vietnam lost more than one million soldiers. North Vietnam lost between 500,000 and a million soldiers.

MARCHING FOR PEACE

The Vietnam War was tearing the United States apart. As the nightly news counted the deaths of American soldiers, more people demanded that America pull its surviving soldiers out. First, university students protested the war. Then, citizens of all ages spoke out, including Martin Luther King Jr.

King was angry that the US government was sending young African American men "8,000 miles (12,800 km) away to guarantee liberties in south-east Asia which they had not found in south-west Georgia or east Harlem."

The **protest** marches were called 'peace marches'. But they were often not peaceful. On 21 October 1967, more than 75,000 people marched outside the Pentagon (US defence headquarters) building in Washington, DC. Soldiers and police arrived to try to control the angry crowd. Soldiers beat about 14,000 protesters with batons and arrested 7000.

> **History of Vietnam**
> **1950** The US begins to send supplies to help the French in a war to keep Vietnam as a French colony
> **1954** The Vietnamese defeat the French. Vietnam is divided into North and South Vietnam.
> **1965** President Johnson sends US Marines to help South Vietnam against **communist** North Vietnam
> **1969** President Nixon begins to withdraw American troops
> **1973** All sides agree to stop fighting. The last US ground troops leave.
> **1975** South Vietnam loses to North Vietnam. North and South Vietnam unite.

▶ The illustration shows an anti-war **demonstration**. By the end of 1967, only 26 per cent of Americans supported sending Americans to the war.

▼ In spring 1970, students at Kent State University in Ohio protested against the war. On 4 May, soldiers threw cans of smoky tear gas into a crowd of students. The students threw them back. Then the soldiers fired their rifles, killing four students.

▲ On 17 March 1973, Robert Strim returned from Vietnam where he had been a prisoner of war. This photo shows the joy of his family as they greeted him at Travis Air Force Base in California.

Leaving Vietnam

In 1968, Republican Richard Nixon was elected president of the United States. He promised to take American troops out of Vietnam. He planned for American soldiers to train South Vietnamese soldiers so they could continue to fight their own war. This plan was called Vietnamization. The US began to withdraw troops in July 1969, but the bombings and fighting continued. Finally, on 29 March 1973, the last US soldiers left Vietnam.

North and South Vietnam continued to fight. North Vietnam finally took over the country. In April 1975, South Vietnam gave up the battle. Then, North Vietnam and South Vietnam became a united Communist country. For the first time, the US could not claim victory in war.

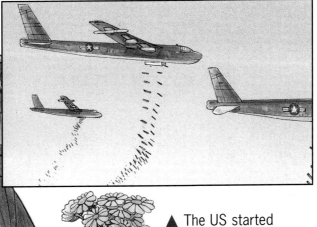

▲ The US started Operation Rolling Thunder in the spring of 1965. It was a huge air attack on North Vietnam. If US B-52 bombers dropped enough bombs, the North Vietnamese might surrender. Rolling Thunder lasted until the autumn of 1968.

▲ Napalm is an explosive petroleum jelly. It causes disastrous fires and terrible human casualties. US planes dropped napalm over jungles where the North Vietnamese enemy hid. Napalm fires ruined huge areas of jungle and countless villages.

THE DREAM UNDER FIRE

"Blacks had been demanding freedom for six years and had gotten nothing. What we're going to start saying now is Black Power!" A young Black leader named Stokely Carmichael shouted these words before a crowd in Mississippi. Soon the crowd was chanting with him: "BLACK POWER! BLACK POWER!"

Stokely Carmichael and Martin Luther King Jr began as partners in the fight for **equality**. But Carmichael grew tired of **non-violence**. So did many other Blacks. In the summers of 1967 and 1968, **riots** broke out in many cities. Many African Americans were frustrated by the low wages they were paid. They were frustrated that prices of food and rents were higher in their neighbourhoods than in White communities. Armed with rocks and Black Power flags, they broke shop windows and burned buildings.

A last speech

On 3 April 1968, Dr King spoke to a crowd in Memphis, Tennessee: "Like anybody else, I would like to live a long life. But I'm not concerned about that now. I just want to do God's will. And He's allowed me to go up to the mountain...and I've seen the Promised Land. I may not get there with you, but I want you to know tonight that we as a people will get to the Promised Land."

King meant that the day for equality and harmony was coming. He just did not think he would be there to see it. The next day, as King was leaving his motel room, he was shot dead.

▶ At 6:00 P.M. on April 4, 1968, Dr. King stood on the balcony by his motel room, waiting for his friends. Across the parking lot, a White man named James Earl Ray pointed a gun at him and shot. At 7:05 P.M., King was dead. In more than 60 American cities, angry African Americans rioted once more.

▲ At the 1968 Olympic Games held in Mexico City, 200-metre-sprint winning US athletes Tommy Smith (centre) and John Carlos (right) gave the black-gloved, clenched-fist Black Power salute.

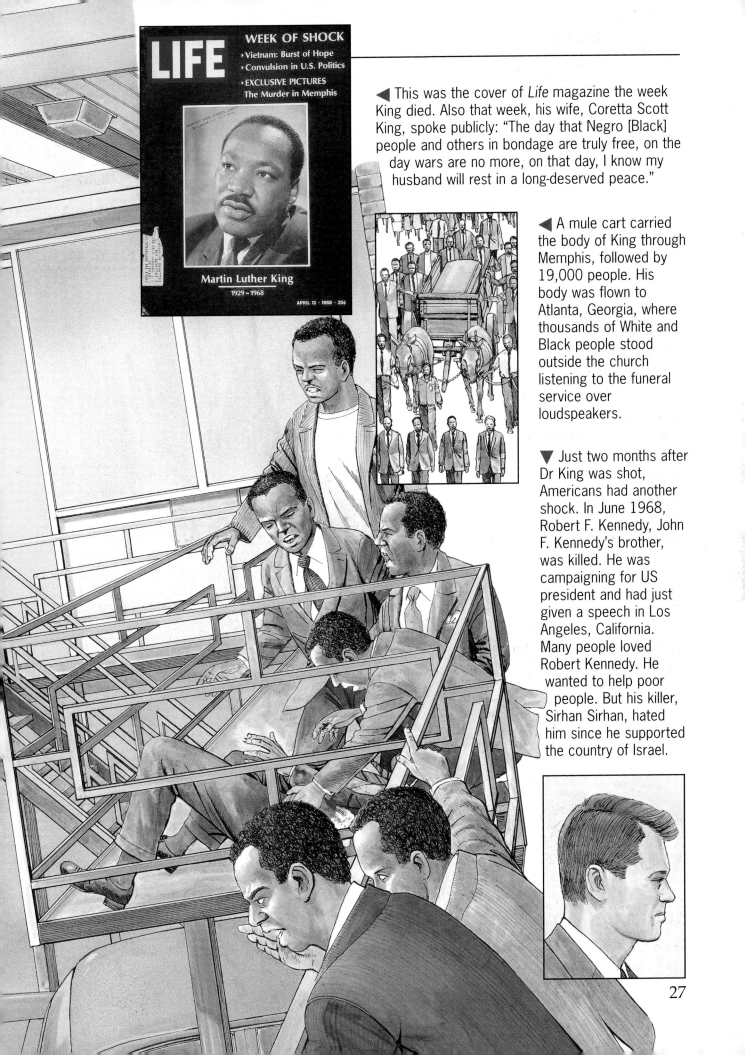

LIFE

WEEK OF SHOCK
›Vietnam: Burst of Hope
›Convulsion in U.S. Politics
›EXCLUSIVE PICTURES
The Murder in Memphis

Martin Luther King
1929 ~ 1968

APRIL 12 · 1968 · 35¢

◀ This was the cover of *Life* magazine the week King died. Also that week, his wife, Coretta Scott King, spoke publicly: "The day that Negro [Black] people and others in bondage are truly free, on the day wars are no more, on that day, I know my husband will rest in a long-deserved peace."

◀ A mule cart carried the body of King through Memphis, followed by 19,000 people. His body was flown to Atlanta, Georgia, where thousands of White and Black people stood outside the church listening to the funeral service over loudspeakers.

▼ Just two months after Dr King was shot, Americans had another shock. In June 1968, Robert F. Kennedy, John F. Kennedy's brother, was killed. He was campaigning for US president and had just given a speech in Los Angeles, California. Many people loved Robert Kennedy. He wanted to help poor people. But his killer, Sirhan Sirhan, hated him since he supported the country of Israel.

27

AMERICANS ON THE MOON

Throughout history, explorers have ventured into unknown lands. With few such places left on Earth, explorers headed into outer space. In 1969, two Americans landed on the Moon. They left a sign there that said: "We came in peace for all mankind."

On 16 July 1969, Apollo 11 blasted off from Cape Kennedy, Florida. It carried three astronauts: Neil Armstrong, Edwin Aldrin Jr and Michael Collins. For four days, they hurtled towards the Moon. Collins recalled what it was like to see the Moon from the spacecraft window: "The Moon I have known all my life, that two-dimensional small yellow disc in the sky, has gone away somewhere, to be replaced by the most awesome sphere I have ever seen. It is huge, completely filling our window. The belly of it bulges out towards us. I almost feel I can reach out and touch it."

Journeys into space
1961 Alan Shepard Jr goes into space
1962 John Glenn Jr orbits Earth
1968 Apollo 8 orbits the Moon
1969 Apollo 11 lands on the Moon
1972 Apollo 17 makes the last manned Moon landing
1973 US launches Skylab space station with astronauts and scientists to study weather and plant growth
1975 The US and **Soviet Union** launch first international manned space mission
1976 *Viking 1* and *2* land on Mars, without astronauts
1977 *Voyager 2* is launched to photograph Jupiter, Saturn, Uranus and Neptune

◀ Apollo 9 was launched on 3 March 1969, with astronauts James McDivitt, David Scott and Russell Schweikart. The mission tested the equipment and procedures to be used in the Moon landing later that year.

▶ Armstrong and Aldrin collected rock samples from the Moon and took photographs. Aldrin said: "This has been far more than three men on a mission to the Moon.... We feel this stands as a symbol of the [never-ending] curiosity of all mankind to explore the unknown."

Younger voters
In 1971, the US passed the 26th **Amendment**. The voting age requirement was lowered from 21 to 18 years old.

A giant leap

On 20 July, Armstrong and Aldrin landed on the Moon. Collins continued to **orbit** in one section of the spacecraft. Aldrin reported: "We opened the hatch and Neil began backing out of the tiny opening. It seemed like a small eternity before I heard Neil say, 'That was one small step for man...one giant leap for mankind'." The two astronauts collected samples of rocks that were 3.7 billion years old. After 21 hours and 36 minutes, their spacecraft lifted off and hooked up with Collins's craft. On 24 July, the three men made a safe splashdown in the Pacific Ocean.

► The 110-storey Sears Tower in Chicago was built in 1973, becoming the world's tallest building at the time.

THE OIL CRISIS

"If your licence plate starts with an even number, you can't buy petrol today." This is how petrol stations controlled their limited supplies of petrol during the oil crisis of the 1970s. Then, Americans could not drive long distances for a holiday. They gave each other lifts to work. How did the oil crisis happen?

By the 1970s, Americans used oil in nearly every part of their lives. Millions of cars, lorries, buses and vans ran on petrol made from crude oil. Fuel oil heated homes, schools and factories. All the newest plastic items were made from oil products. Unfortunately, America did not have enough oil to meet its needs.

The Arab–Israeli conflict

Until 1973, America bought millions of barrels of oil from **Arab nations** in the Middle East. The oil was cheap and plentiful. The Arab nations were fighting an on-going war with their neighbour, Israel. Because the United States supported Israel, the Arab nations decided to cut their shipments of oil to the US.

Threats to factories

The Arab nations raised the price of their oil, too. Suddenly, America had an oil shortage. Many factories closed because they did not have enough heating fuel. Others stayed opened and charged more for their products to cover the higher cost of running the factory.

▶ Drivers queued up to buy petrol when they found a station open. One New Jersey petrol station had a queue that stretched 6.5 km long. Some states made petrol stations close on Sundays. Others limited the amounts of petrol they sold to each customer to make supplies last longer.

◀ On 28 March 1979, there was a failure in the cooling system at the **nuclear** power plant on Three-Mile Island in Pennsylvania. Dangerous **radioactive** gases escaped into the air. If workers had not noticed the failure, a deadly explosion would have occurred just 30 minutes later. Here, a nuclear power station worker checks the radioactivity in nearby Middletown, Pennsylvania.

▼ Americans celebrated the first Earth Day on 22 April 1970. People like these children gathered in towns and cities to **demonstrate** and speak out against the **pollution** of the air and water.

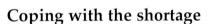

Coping with the shortage

President Nixon ordered all US government buildings to lower their central heating temperatures to save fuel. He encouraged Americans to do the same in their homes and offices. He also signed a law to lower the driving speed limit to 88 km an hour. Slower driving burned less petrol, making less pollution.

Many **environmentalists** warned Americans to stop depending on other countries for oil. They outlined several plans to use less fuel and to develop other energy sources, such as solar (from the Sun) and wave power from the sea.

THE PRESIDENT STEPS DOWN

Richard M. Nixon was president of the United States from 1969 to 1974. He ended America's involvement in Vietnam. He improved America's friendships with other countries. But Nixon is most remembered for one thing. He was the only president who was forced to resign from office by public pressure.

For 21 years, the United States and China (a **communist** country) were enemies. Many Americans were surprised when Nixon visited China in 1972. He believed the leaders of powerful countries must communicate with each other. Nixon also visited the **Soviet Union** and made agreements with its leader. The two leaders agreed to limit the number of weapons they built. This would save the US money and make the world safer.

The Watergate break-in

In 1972, Nixon was running for a second term as president. Men working on his **election** team broke into the offices of his opponents. The offices were in the Watergate building in Washington, DC. The burglars tried to find information that could help Nixon win the election. When the men were caught, Nixon said he did not know about the break-in plans.

Nixon also tried to stop the government from finding out more about the incident. After two years of investigation, it became clear that Nixon and his aides were involved in the break-in. **Congress** prepared to impeach the president, or put him on trial. Nixon decided to resign, or give up, the presidency.

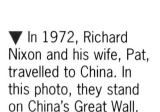 ▼ In 1972, Richard Nixon and his wife, Pat, travelled to China. In this photo, they stand on China's Great Wall.

▲ Many Americans marched around the White House to support Nixon's impeachment for **obstructing justice**.

Who becomes president?

In 1973, Vice President Spiro Agnew resigned because he was accused of accepting **bribes**. The 25th **Amendment** says the president must select, and **Congress** must approve, a new vice president if the serving one leaves office. Gerald Ford, a leader in the House of Representatives, was appointed vice president. When Nixon resigned, Ford became president.

◀ On 9 August 1974, Nixon boarded a helicopter to leave the White House. The day before, he spoke to Americans: "If some of my judgments were wrong – and some were wrong – they were made in what I believed at the time to be in the best interest of the nation."

▼ This Vietnam Veterans Memorial in Washington, DC, lists the names of more than 58,000 Americans who died in the war or who were still missing in action.

EQUALITY FOR WOMEN

Today, women can become doctors, lawyers, police officers and headteachers. Until the 1960s, mostly men held jobs like these. Women were expected to stay home, whether they wanted to or not. Women of the 1960s began to question this. They wanted to use their skills and talents to fulfil their dreams.

In the 1960s, millions of women decided to find interesting and rewarding jobs. The jobs did not come easily. Many law schools and medical schools chose male applicants over female applicants. Many employers thought men were more responsible than women. If women were employed, they were given lower-paid jobs. In 1970, a young woman with a university education earned an average of $6700 a year. A young man educated to the same level earned almost $12,000.

A fight for equality

In the 1960s, women held marches and gave speeches across the United States. In 1963, **Congress** passed a law that said women and men must receive the same pay for doing the same job. The Civil Rights Act of 1964 said that women could not be denied jobs just because they were women.

Many people wanted the Equal Rights **Amendment** added to the Constitution. It would guarantee equal treatment for men and women. In 1972, Congress approved the amendment. But it could not become law without the approval of 38 state governments. Only 35 passed it, so it did not become an amendment.

▲ ▶ These buttons from the 1970s were worn by women who wanted **equality**. NOW, the National Organization of Women, supported raising women's wages and the right of women to make policy, or decisions, in the workplace.

▼ In the 1960s and 1970s, many women still chose to stay home and take full responsibility for cooking, cleaning and child care. Others studied for jobs outside the home, for example scientists and teachers.

Scientist

Teacher

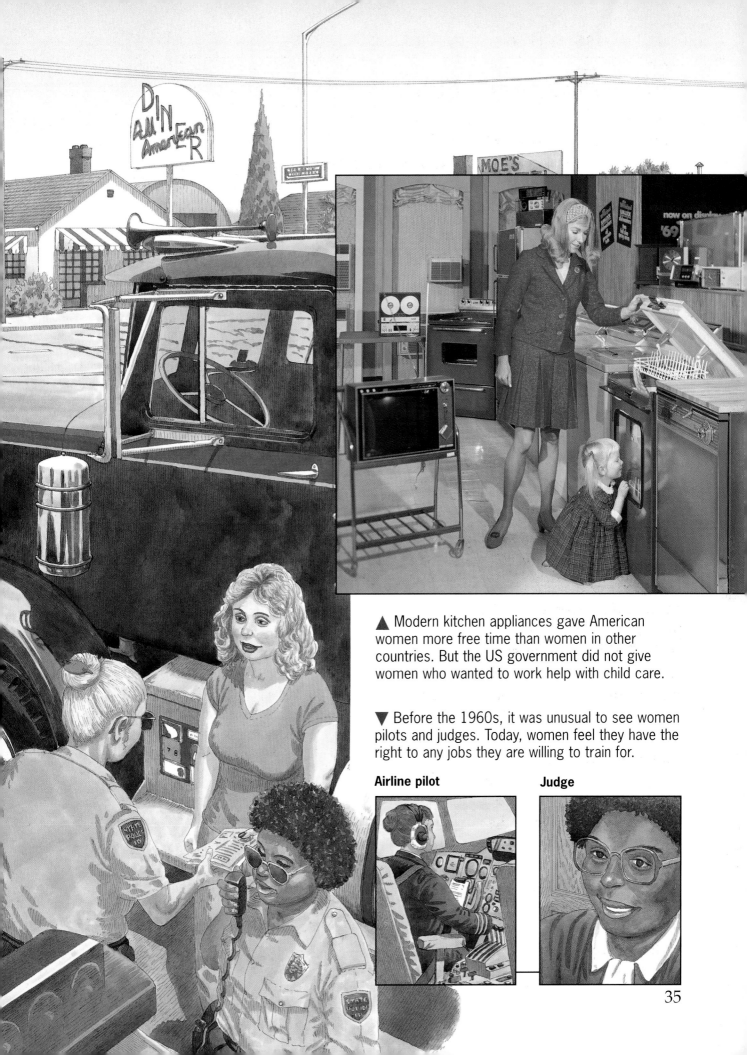

▲ Modern kitchen appliances gave American women more free time than women in other countries. But the US government did not give women who wanted to work help with child care.

▼ Before the 1960s, it was unusual to see women pilots and judges. Today, women feel they have the right to any jobs they are willing to train for.

Airline pilot

Judge

35

HEALTHIER AMERICANS

In 1920, the average person in the US could expect to live to be about 54 years old. By 1970, the average person lived to about age 70. Thanks to discoveries in medicine, and more information about good health, Americans keep living longer and staying healthier.

If you lived in the 1950s, you would have seen TV ads for cigarettes. Many people smoked cigarettes in offices, restaurants and aeroplanes. Then, in the 1960s, scientists reported that cigarette smoke could cause many illnesses. In 1965, **Congress** passed a law requiring a health warning on cigarette packets. In 1971, radio and TV ads for cigarettes were banned. Since then, many states banned smoking in public places.

Progress in medicine
In the 1960s and 1970s, US scientists invented medical equipment to explore the body and repair damaged parts. These included scanners and devices that can see inside the body, an artificial heart, and new, safer types of vaccines.

▶ In a US hospital in the early 1970s, doctors perform a heart transplant on an adult patient. On 3 December 1967, a South African doctor, Christiaan Barnard, performed the world's first heart-transplant operation. He connected the heart from an accident victim into the body of a patient dying of heart disease.

Since then, US doctors increasingly advised Americans to keep their hearts healthy by not smoking, by exercising and by eating less fat and more fruits and vegetables.

▶ This photograph was taken by Charles E. Rotkin in New Orleans, Louisiana, in 1963. A doctor is using a computer to look at an enlarged section of the X-ray picture shown on the screen to his right. With increasing use of computers during the 1970s, medical science and technology developed rapidly.

36

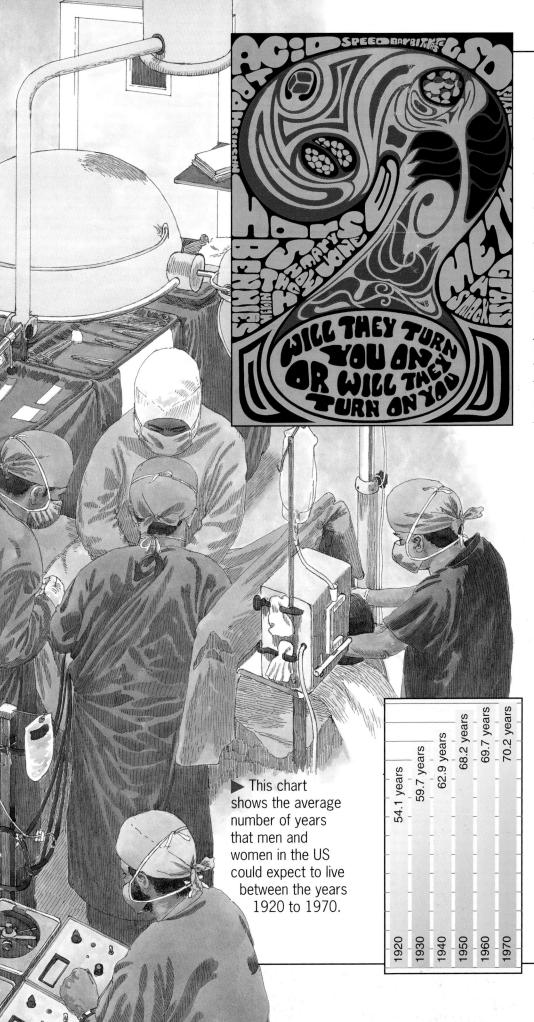

This is an anti-drug poster of the 1970s. These posters tried to warn people of the dangers of drugs. During the 1960s, many young people experimented with drugs. They felt drugs gave them freedom. However, many people paid a terrible price for taking drugs. They failed in their education and at their jobs. They committed crimes. Thousands died from drugs, including famous musicians such as Jimi Hendrix, Janis Joplin and Elvis Presley.

▼ Doctors now use machines like this to look at tissues inside the body. The machine has a huge magnet that sends signals to a computer screen. The machine helps doctors find injuries and diseases. This type of body 'scanner' was developed in the 1970s.

▶ This chart shows the average number of years that men and women in the US could expect to live between the years 1920 to 1970.

	54.1 years	59.7 years	62.9 years	68.2 years	69.7 years	70.2 years
	1920	1930	1940	1950	1960	1970

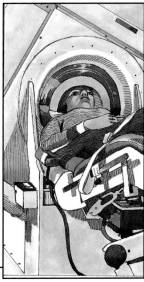

SHOPPING MALL AMERICA

In 1876, shops were located in the centre of town. People lived close enough to walk to the shops. As buses and cars became popular, people moved away from the town-centre. By 1976, the shops had moved out to the suburban communities.

By the 1970s, shoppers no longer worried about bad weather or finding a parking space. Nearly every town had at least one covered shopping mall.

These were still the days before chains of giant bookshops and hardware stores. However, there were many large department and discount stores. The average American earned – and spent – much more money than in the 1950s. There were many more goods to buy.

Buying foreign products

Throughout its history, the US always sold goods to other countries. This is called exporting. It also imported, or bought goods from other countries. Starting in 1976, the US imported more than it exported. Because of the petrol shortage, many Americans bought small, foreign cars, such as the Volkswagen Beetle from Germany and the Toyota Corolla from Japan.

Some US businesses imported clothing and shoes. A man named Philip Knight began importing running shoes from Japan to start a company called Nike. Products like these cost less to make because factory workers in other countries are paid less than US workers.

▲ This is a computer tape storage room in a government building in 1974. Throughout the 1970s, computers were made increasingly smaller. Businesses used computers, but you would rarely see them in homes.

▶ People drove to shopping malls to buy food, clothes and the newest items. Going shopping became a regular family outing. Some city-centre shops could not compete with the shopping malls and went out of business.

◀ These were the latest gadgets of the early 1970s. Pocket calculators and digital watches showed numbers with LCDs (liquid crystal displays). In 1974, 12 million pocket calculators were sold. They cost about $15 each.

◀ Roller skating was as popular in the 1970s as it is today. In the mid-1970s, skates began to have plastic wheels instead of wood or metal ones. This photograph was taken in 1974 in New York.

America's 200th Birthday

On 4 July 1776, America declared its independence from Britain. Then, Americans struggled to write and accept a Constitution. They struggled through the Civil War and two world wars. Through conflicts over slavery, equality and so much more, the United States of America survived and thrived.

On 4 July 1976, America turned 200 years old. It was called the Bicentennial. The celebrations began on 4 July at 4:31 am at Mars Hill, Maine. The Sun rises there before any other place in the US.

As the Sun rose over Fort McHenry in Baltimore, a crowd sang *The Star Spangled Banner*, the US national anthem. People in the town of George, Washington, baked a cherry pie measuring 5.6 sq m. The townsfolk of Boston, Massachusetts, made a 200-cm-diameter pancake. In Sheboygan, Wisconsin, 1776 Frisbees were tossed into the air. In Washington DC, laser lights spelled out '1776–1976, Happy Birthday USA', and Queen Elizabeth II danced with Gerald Ford, the president of the US.

▶ On 4 July, millions of New Yorkers watched Operation Sail from rooftops, windows and river banks.

In addition to the 'Tall Ships', there were 53 warships and more than 200 other ships. They came from such places as Britain, Portugal, Israel, Venezuela, Colombia and Greece.

This event took 20 years to plan. Some Tall Ships set out in May 1976 to cross the Atlantic Ocean to join the celebration. The word 'bicentennial' means two centuries, or 200 years.

▶ By 1976, newly developed Boeing 747 jumbo jet aircraft took people across the Atlantic Ocean in less than 10 hours. What an improvement over the more than 25 days it took to travel by ship in the late 1700s. Now, Americans were travelling all over the world, for holidays as well as for business.

▲ At the end of the day, the Tall Ships docked in New York City harbour, but the festivities continued. A service was held at nearby St Paul's Chapel. In 1789, George Washington and John Quincy Adams worshipped there after their **inauguration** as America's first president and vice president. At 9.00 pm, a spectacular display of fireworks exploded over the Statue of Liberty. Bright lights lit up the statue, as 3000 pieces of fireworks were set off from six sites on Liberty Island and Ellis Island, and on nearby boats.

Operation Sail 1976

The people of New York City were treated to a most spectacular sight. Over 300 ships paraded up the Hudson River. The grandest were called the Tall Ships. They were sixteen of the world's largest sailing vessels. The largest, from Russia, was 113 m long. Several dozen nations sent ships across the ocean for Operation Sail. As these ships made their journey to New York, they passed many ports along the East Coast. Every day, Americans sailed out to greet them in their small sailboats and motor boats. This was a time for everyone to join the nation's 200th birthday party.

Historical Map of America

On the map

This map shows the United States in 1976. Like today, the nation included 50 states and the **commonwealth** of Puerto Rico. The population was more than 200 million. Only India, China and the Soviet Union had more people. Only the **Soviet Union**, Canada and China had more land.

The United States was producing more goods and services than any other nation. There were more than 250 metropolitan areas – cities surrounded by **suburbs**. The largest metropolitan areas were, like today, those around New York City in New York, Los Angeles in California and Chicago in Illinois. Highways (motorways) linked cities and towns throughout the country. Ships came and went from the nation's busy ports.

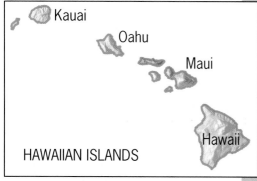

HAWAIIAN ISLANDS

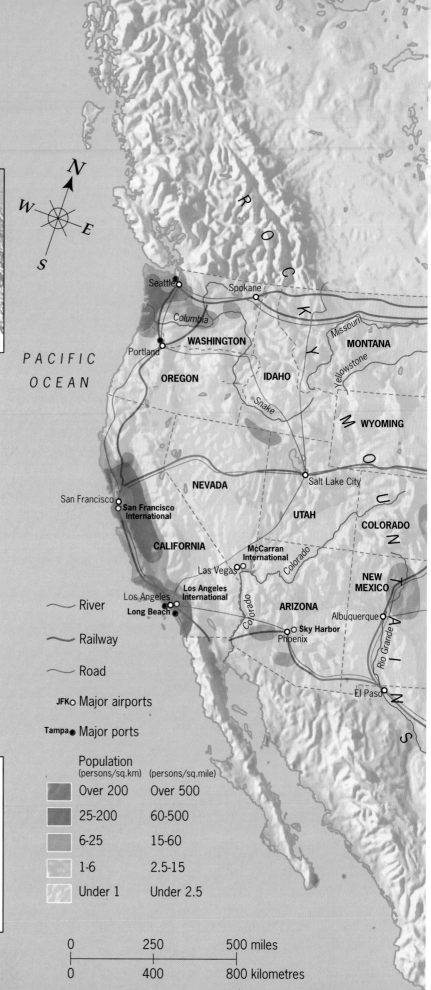

Hudson Bay

CANADA

MAINE

Lake Superior

MINNESOTA

NORTH DAKOTA

Duluth-Superior

Lake Champlain

VERMONT

NEW HAMPSHIRE

Lake Huron

Lake Ontario

NEW YORK

Albany

MASSACHUSETTS

Boston

Logan International

Minneapolis-St. Paul International

St. Paul

WISCONSIN

Sheboygan

MICHIGAN

Buffalo

RHODE ISLAND

CONNECTICUT

Minneapolis

St. Lawrence

BLACK HILLS

SOUTH DAKOTA

Milwaukee

Lake Michigan

Detroit Metropolitan

Detroit

Lake Erie

Cleveland

Kent

PENNSYLVANIA

Pittsburgh

Philadelphia

Chester

Baltimore

JFK

Hudson

New York City

Statue of Liberty

Newark International

NEW JERSEY

IOWA

Chicago

Chicago O'Hare

ILLINOIS

INDIANA

OHIO

Three Mile Island

DELAWARE

WASHINGTON D.C.

NEBRASKA

Indianapolis

Cincinnati

WEST VIRGINIA

Richmond

MARYLAND

Omaha

Missouri

Mississippi

Lambert-St. Louis International

St. Louis

Ohio

Huntington

VIRGINIA

Norfolk Harbor

Missouri

KENTUCKY

APPALACHIAN MOUNTAINS

Kansas City

KANSAS

MISSOURI

NORTH CAROLINA

OKLAHOMA

TENNESSEE

SOUTH CAROLINA

Little Rock

Memphis

Oklahoma City

ARKANSAS

Birmingham

Atlanta

Hartsfield International

Mississippi

Selma

Dallas/Fort Worth International

Montgomery

GEORGIA

ATLANTIC OCEAN

Fort Worth

Dallas

MISSISSIPPI

Jackson

ALABAMA

Jacksonville

TEXAS

LOUISIANA

FLORIDA

Austin

Baton Rouge

Mobile

Pascagoula

Cape Canaveral

San Antonio

Houston

Lake Charles

New Orleans

Orlando International

Port Arthur

Texas City

Tampa

Rio Grande

Corpus Christi

Miami

Miami International

GULF OF MEXICO

MEXICO

CUBA

Famous People of the Time

Ralph Abernathy,
1926–1990, worked with Martin Luther King Jr in organizing boycotts and other civil rights actions. When King died, Abernathy took over the leadership of the Southern Christian Leadership Conference.

Edwin Aldrin Jr,
1930–, was the second person to walk on the Moon. He and Neil Armstrong landed there in Apollo 11 on 20 July 1969.

Neil Armstrong,
1930–, was a US astronaut who became the first person on the Moon in 1969.

Christiaan Barnard,
1922–, performed the first heart-transplant operation in 1967 at the Groote Schuur Hospital in Cape Town, South Africa.

Leonid Brezhnev,
1906–1982, became the leader of the Soviet Union in 1964.

Stokely Carmichael,
1941–1998, was a leader of the Black Power movement. He encouraged African Americans to gain business roles in their communities and to meet violence with violence.

Cesar Chavez,
1927–1993, organized farm workers into a union in an effort to gain better pay and working conditions.

Fidel Castro,
1927–, became the communist leader of Cuba in 1959. He was involved in the Cuban Missile Crisis of 1962.

Michael Collins,
1930–, was an astronaut on the Apollo 11 mission which landed on the Moon.

Dwight D. Eisenhower,
1890–1969, was the 34th president of the US from 1953 to 1961. Before that, he was the Allied Commander in World War II.

Gerald Ford,
1913–, was appointed US vice president in 1973 and became president when Nixon resigned in 1974.

John Glenn Jr,
1921–, became the first American to orbit the Earth in 1962. He made another space flight in 1998.

Ho Chi Minh,
1890–1969, was the first president of North Vietnam from 1954 to 1969.

Lyndon B. Johnson,
1908–1973, as president set up the Great Society plan to help poor people. He was criticized for sending US soldiers to Vietnam.

John F. Kennedy,
1917–1963, was the youngest president elected in the US. He was assassinated in Dallas.

Important Dates and Events

EVENTS IN THE UNITED STATES 1950 to 1961

1950–1953 US troops fight the Korean War
1951 22nd Amendment set two-term limit for presidents
1951 the first *I Love Lucy* show runs on TV
1952 the first edition of *Mad Comics* goes on sale
1952 the United Nations building in New York City holds its first session
1954 in *Brown v. Board of Education*, the Supreme Court rules that separate schools for African Americans are against the law
1954 Dr Jonas Salk announces a vaccine to prevent the disease polio
1955 Rosa Parks is arrested for refusing to give up her seat on a bus to a White person
1955 Disneyland opens in California
1959 first US soldiers (acting as advisors) are killed in Vietnam
1959 Alaska and Hawaii become states
1960 23rd Amendment gives residents of Washington, DC the right to vote in presidential elections
1960 Nixon–Kennedy debates are seen on television
1961 Alan Shepard becomes the first American in space on 5 May

EVENTS IN THE UNITED STATES 1962 to 1976

1962 John Glenn Jr becomes the first American in orbit
1963 President Kennedy is assassinated
1964 Congress passes Civil Rights Act
1964 the 24th Amendment bans poll taxes which demand people to pay money in order to vote
1965 US combat troops enter Vietnam
1965 riots break out in the Watts section of Los Angeles, California
1965 Cesar Chavez organizes farm workers to stop working for grape growers and college students to stop buying grapes
1966 Betty Friedan helps organize the National Organization of Women
1967 the 25th Amendment sets rules for replacing the president and vice president if they die, become disabled or leave office
1968 Senator Robert Kennedy is assassinated
1969 Americans land on the Moon
1971 the 26th Amendment lowers the voting age from 21 to 18 years
1973 last US troops leave Vietnam
1974 President Nixon resigns
1976 America celebrates its 200th birthday

Robert Kennedy, 1925–1968, was the attorney general when his brother John was president. He was assassinated during his campaign for president.

Nikita Khrushchev, 1894–1971, was the leader of the Soviet Union from 1955 to 1964.

Martin Luther King Jr, 1929–1968, was a powerful leader in the civil rights movement. He encouraged non-violent activities as the way to achieve equality among the races.

Henry Kissinger, 1923–, advised presidents Nixon and Ford on foreign policy. He won the Nobel Peace Prize in 1973 for arranging the ceasefire in Vietnam.

Malcolm X, 1925–1965, was an African American leader who thought his people should create their own society. He was assassinated in 1965.

Joseph McCarthy, 1908–1957, was a US senator from Wisconsin. In the 1950s, he accused many government officials and others of being communists.

Richard M. Nixon, 1913–1994, was the first US president to resign. He is remembered for ending US involvement in Vietnam and opening communications between the US, China and the Soviet Union.

Rosa Parks, 1913–, was very active in seeking civil rights for all African Americans. She is best known for refusing to give up her seat on a bus to White passengers. This led to a bus boycott in Montgomery, Alabama, and to the beginning of a major civil rights movement.

Elvis Presley, 1935–1977, became the most popular American rock 'n roll singer. He also appeared in 32 motion pictures.

Alan Shepard Jr, 1923–1998, became the first American in space in 1961. In 1971, he became the fifth astronaut to set foot on the Moon.

Norman Shumway, 1923–, performed America's first heart-transplant operation on an adult patient on 6 January 1968.

Frank Sinatra, 1915–1998, was among America's and the world's most famous singers of popular music between the late 1940s and the 1970s.

Harry Truman, 1884–1972, was the 33rd president of the US from 1945 to 1953. He made one of the most important presidential decision: to drop two atomic bombs on Japan to end World War II.

US presidents from 1948 to 1976
Harry S. Truman
1945–1953
Dwight D. Eisenhower
1953–1961
John F. Kennedy
1961–1963
Lyndon B. Johnson
1963–1969
Richard M. Nixon
1969–1974
Gerald R. Ford
1974–1977

MARTIN LUTHER KING Jr
1929 born in Atlanta, Georgia, on 15 January
1947 becomes a Baptist minister
1948 graduates from Morehouse College
1953 marries Coretta Scott
1954 becomes pastor of Dexter Avenue Baptist Church in Montgomery, Alabama
1955 earns PhD in religion from Boston University
1957 elected President of Southern Christian Leadership Conference (SCLC)
1963 delivers 'I Have a Dream' speech in Washington, DC
1964 awarded the Nobel Peace Prize
1965 leads marches and demonstrations in Selma, Alabama
1966 moves with family to poor neighbourhood in Chicago and leads demonstrations
1968 leads demonstrations in Memphis, Tennessee; is assassinated in Memphis on April 4

THE REST OF NORTH AND SOUTH AMERICA
1946 Juan Peron becomes President of Argentina
1949 Newfoundland becomes part of Canada
1959 Fidel Castro takes over Cuba's government
1960 Brasilia becomes the new capital city of Brazil
1962 Cuban Missile Crisis
1962 Jamaica, Trinidad and Tobago gain independence from Britain
1966 Guyana and Barbados gain independence from Britain
1967 Che Guevara, leader of communist forces in Bolivia, is killed
1973 US supports a military takeover in Chile to replace the elected leader, President Allende

THE REST OF THE WORLD
1948 Mohandas Gandhi is assassinated in India
1948 Israel declares itself an independent Jewish state
1949 The US, Canada and ten western European nations create the North Atlantic Treaty Organization (NATO)
1949 Mao Zedong creates the communist People's Republic of China
1957 The Soviet Union launches *Sputnik I*, the first space satellite
1953 Edmund Hillary and Tenzing Norgay conquer Mount Everest, the highest mountain in the world
1956 Soviet tanks enter Hungary to stop threat to communist government
1961 Soviet cosmonaut Yuri Gagarin becomes the first human in space
1964 Nelson Mandela is sentenced to life in prison for trying to protest against the South African government
1975 the Vietnam War ends with a victory for communist North Vietnam

GLOSSARY

amendment change in a document, such as the US Constitution

Arab nations countries whose native language is Arabic. They are in the Middle East.

boycott refuse to buy something

bribe money offered to persuade someone to do something for you

capitalism an economic system in which individuals or companies can own businesses, fix prices of goods and keep wealth and land

civil rights personal freedoms of citizens

commonwealth nation or state that is governed by its people; Puerto Rico is a commonwealth of the US. Puerto Ricans are US citizens, but cannot vote in presidential elections.

communist way of organizing a country so that all businesses and land belong to the government and the profits are shared by everyone

Congress part of US government that makes laws

conscripted require someone to serve in the military

debate discussion between sides with different views

democratic way of organizing a country so that the people can elect their leaders

demonstration gathering of people who want to show their opinions together

discrimination unfair or unequal treatment of a person or group

election process of choosing someone by voting

environmentalist person who tries to protect the land and control pollution

equality condition of being equal, especially having equal rights and responsibilities

immigrant person who comes to live in a country from another country

inauguration ceremony to put someone in a position of leadership, like the president of a country

migrant worker person who moves from place to place to find work

missile weapon that is thrown or shot at a target

NAACP National Association for the Advancement of Coloured People

NASA National Aeronautics and Space Administration

non-violent without destruction; peaceful

nuclear to do with energy created by splitting atoms

obstruct justice to stop the truth from coming out

orbit to travel around a planet

pollution harmful materials in the air, water, or soil

poverty being poor

protest to speak out against something publicly

race one of the major groups into which humans are divided; people of the same race have similar looks, such as skin colour

radiation energy sent out from a radioactive material or nuclear reaction

revolution complete change

riot gathering of people who are behaving in a noisy, violent way

segregate to keep separate

slave person who is owned by another person and is usually made to work for that person without payment

Soviet Union country that was once made up of 15 republics in eastern Europe and northern Asia. It was headed by Russia. Also known as the USSR, the Union of Soviet Socialist Republics

suburb small community outside a large city

Supreme Court the highest court in the US

treaty written agreement

unconstitutional goes against the laws or principles of the US Constitution

union group of workers who join together to try to improve working conditions and wages

United Nations group of nations who agree to work together for world peace

MORE BOOKS TO READ

To Kill A Mocking Bird, Harper Lee, Heinemann, Oxford

Tell Me About Martin Luther King, John Hallam, Evans Brothers Ltd, London 1999

African-American Civil Rights, Michael Weber, Evans Brothers Ltd, London 1999

Black Peoples of the Americas, Bob Rees and Marika Sherwood, Heinemann, Oxford

Living Through History: Twentieth Century World, N. Kelly, R. Rees, J. Shuter, Heinemann, Oxford 1999

PLACES TO VISIT

The Imperial War Museum
Horseferry Road
London
SE1 6HZ
Telephone: 020 7416 5000

The American Museum in Britain
Claverton Manor
Bath BA2 7BD
Telephone: 01225 460 503

Merseyside Maritime Museum
Albert Dock
Liverpool L3 4AQ
Telephone: 0151 478 4499

Maritime Heritage Centre
Wapping Wharf
Gas Ferry Road
Bristol BS1 6TY
Telephone: 0117 926 0680

Minority Rights Group
379 Brixton Road,
London SW9 7DE
Telephone: 020 7978 9498
http://www.minorityrights.org

Institute for Race Relations
2–6 Leeke Street,
London WC1X 9HS
Telephone: 020 8837 0041

INDEX

47

INDEX